LOOKING BACK

WEST AFRICAN STATES

BEFORE COLONIALISM

CATHERINE CHAMBERS

Evans

EVANS BROTHERS LIMITED

Evans Brothers Limited
2A Portman Mansions
Chiltern Street
London W1M 1LE

Editor: Nicola Barber
Designer: Neil Sayer
Picture research: Victoria Brooker
Maps: Nick Hawken
Production: Jenny Mulvanny

Consultant: Dr Kevin Shillington

Printed in Spain by GRAFO, S.A. - Bilbao

First published 1999

British Library Cataloguing in Publication Data

Chambers, Catherine
  West African states : from the 15th century to
  colonialism. - (Looking back)
  1.Africa, West - History - To 1884 - Juvenile
  literature
  2.Africa, West - History - 1884-1960 - Juvenile
  literature
  I.Title
  966'.02

ISBN 0237517272

For Anthony King, of course

Acknowledgements

Cover (central image) Werner Forman (background image) J Pate/Robert Harding Picture Library
Title page British Museum/Bridgeman Art Library **page 6** Mary Jelliffe/Hutchison Library **page 7**
Hutchison Library **page 8** Hutchison Library **page 10** Werner Forman **page 11** Betty Press/Panos
Pictures **page 12** Mary Evans Picture Library **page 13** Werner Forman **page 14** Chris
Barton/Christine Osborne Pictures **page 15** Werner Forman **page 16** (top and bottom) Christine
Osborne Pictures **page 19** D Else/Christine Osborne Pictures **page 20** Hutchison Library **page 21**
Betty Press/Panos Pictures **page 23** Werner Forman **page 24** Werner Forman **page 25** Werner
Forman **page 27** Bruce Paton/Panos Pictures **page 28** Royal Albert Memorial Museum,
Exeter/Bridgeman Art Library **page 29** Werner Forman **page 30** Werner Forman **page 31** Mary
Evans Picture Library **page 32** Crispin Hughes/Panos Pictures **page 33** Mary Evans Picture Library
page 34 (top) Werner Forman (bottom) Mary Evans Picture Library **page 35** Thelma Sanders/Panos
Pictures **page 36** Hutchison Library **page 37** Mary Jelliffe/Hutchison Library **page 38** Werner
Forman **page 40** Werner Forman **page 41** Werner Forman **page 42** Werner Forman **page 43** Peter
Newark's Historical Pictures **page 44** (top) Tropix/M & V Birley (bottom) Private Collection/Bridgeman
Art Library **page 45** British Library/Bridgeman Art Library **page 46** Mary Evans Picture Library **page
47** Mary Evans Picture Library **page 48** J Hatt/Hutchison Library **page 49** Mary Evans Picture
Library **page 50** (top) Christina Dodwell/Hutchison Library (bottom) Neil Cooper/Panos Pictures **page
51** Crispin Hughes/Hutchison Library **page 52** Christine Osborne Pictures **page 54** British
Museum/Bridgeman Art Library **page 55** Werner Forman **page 56** (top) Josef Herman
Collection/Bridgeman Art Library (bottom) Werner Forman **page 57** David Reed/Panos Pictures **page
58** Werner Forman **page 59** Mary Evans Picture Library

CONTENTS

INTRODUCTION

West Africa is a huge region that stretches from the Atlantic Ocean in the west to the Bight of Biafra in the east. Its terrain ranges from the southern Sahara and grasslands in the north to the tropical forests and deltas of the coastal regions in the south and west (see map on page 9). It is impossible in such a small space to describe all the states that have come and gone in this vast, complex area. So this book gives examples of types of kingdom and empire from the 15th to the 19th centuries. It looks at how states were organised and run, their economies, and the part played by religion and the arts in people's lives. It reveals the deep contrasts of the area, but also the historical and cultural links that bound it together.

A Tuareg traveller rides through the dry, northern savannah region, beyond the Dyoundé Mountains in modern-day Mali.

INTRODUCTION

HOW DO WE KNOW?

How do we know about the history of this region? First there are the provable facts, for example dates of events, such as battles and the reigns of rulers. These have been agreed by comparing and confirming many different sources. Secondly there are explanations of why or how things happened. Often these accounts raise questions. How did observers, historians or archaeologists arrive at their explanation of events? What assumptions did they make? Most importantly, what kinds of sources did they use and how did they interpret them?

Most of the direct evidence in this book comes from written eyewitness accounts. These accounts and observations, especially those by foreign visitors, can sometimes be clouded by the writer's own customs and expectations. Observers are often influenced by their own interests, or by the interests of the people who will read their accounts.

Oral traditions are an important source in West African history. These are accounts that are passed down through generations by word of mouth. They are usually descriptions of historical events, or genealogies (lists of rulers in chronological order).

A village nestles by a creek on the Niger Delta. Creeks and channels create a complex maze of navigable waterways among the lush, green vegetation of the Delta.

CHAPTER ONE

These traditions are often communicated artistically, as chant, song or poetry. Such accounts may change in subtle ways in order to please a particular audience – for example they may omit shameful events in the history of a society. Oral traditions were obviously important in societies in which people did not read or write, but they were equally as vital in literate societies.

In many parts of Africa, written accounts and archaeological evidence are not available. In places where there are archaeological remains, they are often not sufficient in numbers to produce an accurate picture of a society and events – yet many historians have relied on them to make statements about a whole culture or an era. Another method of trying to reconstruct and understand past practices and lifestyles is to look at present-day customs, ceremonies and artefacts. This study is called social anthropology. Some activities have changed little over many generations, and therefore reveal a lot about the past. However, other activities have been altered by outside influences, and history can sometimes be distorted by trying to understand the past through the present.

Traditionally, the Argungu Festival in northern Nigeria celebrates the fishing harvest, but it also includes both music and poetry.

ORIGINS AND GROWTH

If you look at the maps on pages 18 and 22 you will see that the states examined in this book are spread across a large part of West Africa. Geographical factors affected how and why each state developed. All over the world, settlements need a constant water supply nearby, and the early West African states were no exception. Most states were centred on part of the Niger-Benue river system, the River Volta or the River Senegal. Many thousands of years ago, large-scale agriculture developed near these waterways. As these farming communities became more successful their populations grew.

Large populations prospered in other geographical zones of West Africa. In the savannah

This map shows the main rivers and geographical zones in West Africa.

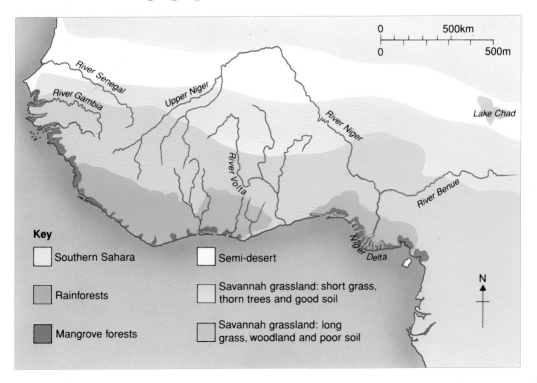

500km

0 — 500m

River Senegal

River Gambia

Upper Niger

River Niger

Lake Chad

River Volta

River Benue

Niger Delta

Key

Southern Sahara

Rainforests

Mangrove forests

Semi-desert

Savannah grassland: short grass, thorn trees and good soil

Savannah grassland: long grass, woodland and poor soil

N

9

grasslands and semi-desert, people cultivated edible crops such as pearl millet, sorghum and rice. They also grew textile crops, such as cotton and a type of hemp. In the forest regions, the kola nut, palm oil, and root crops such as yams were among the many forest products. All of these early populations organised themselves in order to maintain food production, to trade excess produce, and to preserve law and order.

Archaeologists have recovered many artefacts at sites in West Africa. These finds help to paint a picture of an area rich in human activity. Many of the artefacts are made of fine materials. They are beautifully crafted, with exquisite detail. This suggests that they were made for rich people by trained artists. It shows that the organisation of societies in the region had developed to such an extent that people had enough time and wealth to be creative. All of these things indicate that long before the main period dealt with in this book, there were highly organised societies in West Africa.

This bronze shell water vessel was made in Ibo Ukwu, eastern Nigeria, about 1200 years ago. The vessel was cast using the lost wax process (see page 55).

PROBLEMS OF ORIGIN

Evidence from archaeological finds and from other remains shows that early West African states developed as a result of local conditions. However, the oral traditions in many of the states tell a different story. Legends often refer to kingmakers coming from the north and the east. A kingmaker is someone who has the power and influence to appoint people to positions of authority. In their oral traditions, many West African societies mention these kingmakers as the founders of their kingdoms and empires. Some historians agree with these traditions and have suggested that the kingmakers

ORIGINS AND GROWTH

A CLOSER LOOK
Daura is one of the seven Hausa states
(see page 19).
Its legend of origin tells
how all Hausa peoples descended from
Bayajida, son of the king of Baghdad:

One day, Bayajida quarrelled with his
father. He left his homeland and travelled
across Africa until he came to Daura.
There, he found that the local people had
a terrible problem. They could draw water
from their well only on Fridays. On all the
other days, a huge snake with a horse's
head rose up from the well, scaring
everyone away. So Bayajida killed the
snake. The queen of Daura was so
impressed that she married Bayajida, and
they had a son called Bawo. Bawo himself
had six sons, who became the kings of
the other Hausa states.

must have been travellers,
traders or even princes from far
North Africa. It is true that
people have crossed Africa in all
directions for thousands of years
and it is highly likely that there
was contact between West and
North Africa. But other evidence
suggests that West African states
originated on their own,
without the help of kingmakers
from far-off lands.

As agriculture developed
thousands of years ago, farmers
began to grow more produce
than they needed for themselves
or their families. This surplus
was sold, and a trade in crops
developed. It is probable that
goods from the heart of West
Africa reached as far as Egypt.
The evidence also suggests that the West African
states arose from societies that developed
separately, but at the same time, as those of Egypt
and Asia.

*Separating millet
grain from the chaff
at the edge of a field
in Mali*

11

TIMES OF CHANGE

TIMES OF CHANGE

The main period covered by this book was one of change and discovery throughout the world – especially in the Americas and Africa. In West Africa, this period can be divided into three distinct eras: from the 15th to the early 17th century; from the 17th to the early 19th century; and the 19th century itself, leading into the early 20th century.

THE FIRST ERA

By the beginning of the 15th century, there were already many long-established states in West Africa. Some were small kingdoms – others were huge empires. Their origins were ancient and, apart from accounts of legendary kingmakers, are largely unknown (see page 10). But, as in so many parts of

A camel caravan makes its way to the Moroccan city of Marrakech in about 1700. This prosperous city lay at the end of many of the trans-Saharan trade routes.

TIMES OF CHANGE

A Benin craftsworker carved this ivory salt cellar in the 16th century. It shows Portuguese noblemen, with a Portuguese trading vessel on the lid.

the world, these states probably began from the organisation of societies with successful agricultural and trading practices. They expanded over hundreds of years, mainly in order to control more of the trade across the Sahara. From the 8th century AD, this meant trade with the Muslim Moorish people of North Africa. (The Moors were people of mixed Arab and African Berber descent who, in AD 756, established an empire in the regions of Morocco and Algeria.)

Different states played different roles in the trans-Saharan trade. The forest states (Guinea states: see box) to the south of the region supplied the states on the edge of the desert (Sudanic states: see box) with gold, kola nuts, other forest products such as nut oils and gums, and slaves. In return, the Sudanic states made sure their Guinea trading partners received salt, potash, copper, brassware and cloth – exports from the Sudan, North Africa, and from the East.

EUROPEAN EXPLORATIONS

During the 15th century, Portuguese explorers began to take an interest in West Africa. Their eventual aim was to find a southern route around Africa and to trading ports in India, as the Mediterranean Sea and overland routes to the East were largely under Muslim control. However, as they sailed further round the African coast, Portuguese explorers and traders secured trade with the West African gold- and ivory-producing states, such as Benin. In exchange for gold and ivory, the Portuguese offered manufactured goods and firearms. In subsequent years, firearms became increasingly important in West Africa. With guns, it became easier for states to protect themselves from their enemies, and to gain new territory.

While the Portuguese were busy venturing around the African coastline, the Spanish funded a voyage of exploration across the Atlantic Ocean. This led to the 'discovery' by Christopher Columbus of the Americas in 1492. Europeans quickly started to settle and develop this 'New World' for their own ends. The Americas were soon to provide new trading opportunities for European traders and many West African states.

In the 16th century, as the Americas were being developed, and as other European traders began to take an interest in West Africa, some of the larger states just south of the Sahara were invaded by Moorish Moroccan troops from North Africa. The West African powers affected were plunged into decay. Agriculture was disrupted, causing much suffering. As a result, the trans-Saharan trade organised by these states started its slow decline.

Elmina castle was built by the Portuguese on the coast of modern-day Ghana in 1482. At first, the Europeans built forts to try to prevent other European merchants from trading in gold with the coastal states. Later, the forts became prisons for slaves before their transportation to the Americas.

THE SECOND ERA

During the 17th century, European traders and African rulers involved West Africa in a triangular trade network that included European nations, most West African states and the Americas. This trade was based on the export of slaves from West Africa in exchange for European manufactured goods and guns. The slaves were taken to the Americas to work on huge sugar, cotton and tobacco plantations, or in gold and silver mines. This new venture altered the old trading patterns in Africa. Trade between the states of West and North Africa continued to decline. At the same time, the West African states did more business with European trading companies, and European nations slowly gained power in the area. Some of the older West African states collapsed, others prospered, and still others were born.

This wooden headdress was made by an Ibo craftsworker from eastern Nigeria about 100 years ago. It shows a European slave trader and a woman captive.

The West African coast became a hive of activity as new trading states developed. European trading posts and forts were built on the shores of the Atlantic. Manufactured goods and food from Europe and the Americas made their way into the marketplaces of West Africa. Modern firearms gave power to those who had never previously held it.

In many respects this trade led to a slow, relentless decline in West Africa. Slaves were a traditional part of West African society long before the start of the trans-Atlantic slave trade. Usually, they were captives taken during warfare between states. But the normal supply of slaves was insufficient for the demands of the new colonies in the Americas. Many slave-trading states in West Africa started armed conflicts deep in the interior, mostly in order to capture more slaves. Millions of captives were taken and sold as slaves. Moreover, in the Americas, Europeans introduced a new type of slavery never before experienced by West Africans. It was based on unimaginable barbarism and deep humiliation.

15

CHAPTER THREE

THE THIRD ERA

During the 19th century and at the beginning of the 20th century, there was increased conflict between the West African states. Power struggles within many of the states also weakened them. The slave trade was gradually abolished (see page 47) leaving most states with a crumbling economy. Few people in West Africa recognised the growing threat of European powers

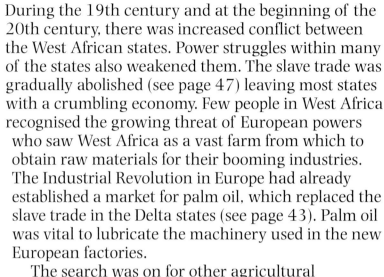

Oil palm kernels (top) are processed into a rich, red oil (bottom). The oil is used for cooking, as well as in industry.

who saw West Africa as a vast farm from which to obtain raw materials for their booming industries. The Industrial Revolution in Europe had already established a market for palm oil, which replaced the slave trade in the Delta states (see page 43). Palm oil was vital to lubricate the machinery used in the new European factories.

The search was on for other agricultural products and natural riches that could be exploited. France and Britain, especially, looked to Africa for raw materials to supply their factories. European

trading companies no longer maintained friendly trade agreements with West African states. Instead, backed by military might, the trading companies forced the states to hand over control of their territories, first to the companies and, later, to the European governments themselves. By the late 19th century, fierce armed struggle by some of the states was still not powerful enough to keep the Europeans out. By 1919, the last of the West African states had lost their independence and the era of colonialism had begun.

LOOKING AT THE STATES

The division of many West African states into Sudanic and Guinea (see page 13) reflects geographical, economic and political similarities. The early Sudanic states grew as a result of their control over the trans-Saharan trade between North Africa and the Guinea states (see page 13). Their ruling classes adopted Islam, the religion of the North African traders. The early Guinea states also developed through trade – but their wealth was gained through the supply of goods to the Sudanic states and North Africa. Between the 17th and 19th centuries, involvement in the Atlantic slave trade allowed some of the Guinea states to expand even further. Unlike the Sudanic leaders, the kings of the Guinea states practised traditional religions (see page 28) and did not adopt Islam, but their methods of rule were probably influenced by Muslim ideas from the north. However, there were many similarities between the two types of state.

It is also useful to remember that many of the larger empires, such as Oyo, included kingdoms within them – so smaller states were often operating, sometimes quite independently, within larger ones. These smaller states are often known as vassal states. They were often required to pay taxes, called tribute, in the form of goods, crops, raw materials and slaves to their powerful overlords.

SOME SUDANIC STATES

1. Mali

Mali is an example of a state that expanded hugely as a result of controlling and extending the trade between West Africa and North Africa. It had its

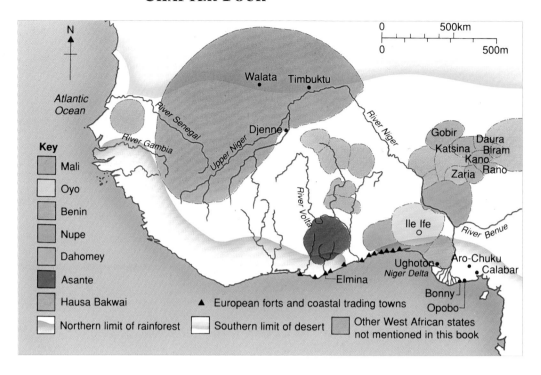

This map shows some of the states and empires mentioned in this chapter at the height of their power.

origins in the 10th century AD when communities of Mande-speaking peoples banded together to form a larger social and political unit. This was the kernel of an empire, which was built on in the following two centuries. Mali was situated originally on the right bank of the Upper Niger. Here, the Mande peoples became rich from agriculture. But Mali became even more wealthy by taking control of the gold trade with North Africa. The gold came from the forest states to the south, was traded in Mali and taxed as it passed through the empire on its route to the north. Great trading towns such as Timbuktu and Walata came under Mali's control.

By the 15th century, Mali had begun to decline as a result of power struggles and attacks from kingdoms under Mali's control. The Songhai Empire expanded around Mali, taking away control of trade routes. The Mande-related Bambara people took

A CLOSER LOOK

Mali had many famous leaders. Sundiata, the 'Lion King', came to power in about 1230. He expanded the empire to the Sahara in the north, modern Senegal in the west and beyond the bend of the the Niger in the east. Following Sundiata's reign, Sabakura and Mansa Musa led Mali to its height in the 14th century. In 1324, Mansa Musa made a famous pilgrimage to Makkah. He travelled across the Sahara, showering gold along the way. When he reached Cairo, his generosity was so great that the value of gold in Egypt dropped dramatically and did not recover for many years!

The huge mosque and market place at Djenne. In the 13th century AD, Djenne was the most important trading centre along the trans-Saharan trade route. It was also a renowned centre for Islamic studies.

over of the shrunken kingdom of Mali and renamed it Segu. In 1861, Segu was taken over by Umar ibn Said Tal's Muslim movement (see page 21). But it remained a disorganised state, and easy prey for French colonialists in the early 20th century.

2. Hausa Bakwai

The Hausa people live to the east of the Niger bend, and north of the place where the Benue and the Niger rivers meet. Since the 10th century, possibly much earlier, Hausa communities organised themselves into well-defended, walled towns. These towns grew into city-states, controlling outlying villages, which provided food and taxes. Power within each state lay with whoever had the authority to organise traditional ceremonies and customs. Yet, for most of this period, the ruling class itself was Muslim.

By the 14th century there were seven Hausa states, known as the Hausa Bakwai ('bakwai' means 'seven'). The best documented of the Hausa Bakwai are Katsina, Kano and Zaria. These seven states never united as an empire – indeed, they quarrelled continually. But the Hausa states were powerful

This is a typical example of architecture in the Hausa states. The patterned plasterwork shows the influence of Muslim decoration.

A CLOSER LOOK

Amina was the queen of the Hausa state of Zaria. She extended her empire as far as the sea in the south and the west, and forced Katsina and Kano to pay tribute to her. She expanded trade, so that goods from far West Africa reached Zaria. She set up walled Hausa trading towns so that craftsworkers – tanners, weavers, smiths, dyers and leatherworkers – found an ever-increasing market for their goods. It is said that Queen Amina took a lover in every town that she conquered – silencing each one before she left by beheading him! Chroniclers cannot agree when this amazing monarch reigned – maybe it was between the 15th and 16th centuries. Historians are unsure whether Zaria's gallant queen was fact or legend. But the Hausa people have no doubt that she was real, and her name lives on in songs composed in her honour.

traders, dominating the trans-Saharan trade when states such as Mali fell into decline. The Hausa also created wealth through their farming and craft manufacturing skills.

3. The Fulani Empire

The Fulani were originally a nomadic people who moved from place to place with their herds of cattle. They came from the area of modern-day Senegal, but from the 14th century onwards they moved eastwards, spreading their grazing territories across the Hausa states and beyond. They did not conquer the people whose lands they moved across. Instead they lived alongside people in settled communities. Eventually some Fulani adopted the farming methods of the settled people and moved into towns and villages. Others continued to live as nomads. In some Fulani

Looking at the States

A CLOSER LOOK

The most renowned of the Fulani leaders, Uthman dan Fodio, sparked a religious revolution in the Hausa states. He was supported not only by Muslim believers but also by followers of traditional religions. These supporters did not necessarily want an Islamic state. But many of the poor hoped that a new leadership would reduce the crippling taxation imposed upon them by the Hausa ruling classes. The Fulani *jihads* created a huge empire covering most of the Benue River to the east and nearly half of the Niger to the west (see map on page 22).

communities, traditional religions continued to be practised, but many Fulani converted to Islam.

In the 18th century, devout Muslim Fulani leaders, and others, started several holy wars, called *jihads*. They wanted to establish states with politics, laws, education and social practices based entirely on Islam. As a result of these *jihads*, Muslim leaders took control of much of western Sudan in the late 18th and early 19th centuries.

By the mid-19th century, a huge Islamic state had been created around the Upper Niger and as far west as the Senegal River. This was the work of two devout Muslims, Sheikh Hamadu and Umar ibn Said Tal. By the 1860s, Umar ibn Said Tal's had empire swallowed up states such as Segu (see page 19).

A Fulani family drives its herd of cattle across the dry savannah of modern-day Mali.

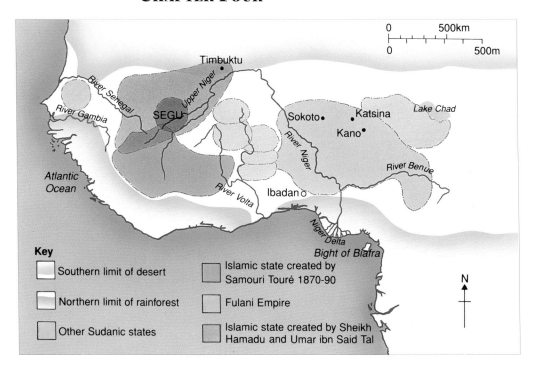

Key

Southern limit of desert	Islamic state created by Samouri Touré 1870-90
Northern limit of rainforest	Fulani Empire
Other Sudanic states	Islamic state created by Sheikh Hamadu and Umar ibn Said Tal

This map shows the Islamic states and empires that resulted from the Fulani jihads.

The aims of the *jihads* were religious and political. The attempt to convert people to Islam was largely successful, and the Fulani rulers gained huge influence. But if another aim was to restart the trans-Saharan trade and the glory of the old Sudanic empires, then it failed. So, too, did the fierce attempts to stop the growing threat from French and British colonialists in the 19th and early 20th centuries.

SOME GUINEA STATES

1. Oyo

The Oyo Empire lay originally in the savannah area, just to the south of the Niger. Like Benin and Dahomey (see pages 23 and 24), the Yoruba people of Oyo took their political and spiritual power from the great early civilisation and religious centre of Ile Ife (see box). Its beginnings are sketchy, but it is thought that the Oyo state emerged some time between the 10th and 14th centuries AD. Oyo was in a powerful trading position between the Sudan and Benin, and it exacted trade duties on goods passing through its territories. Its revenue was also boosted by tribute from smaller, vassal states. Horses and grooms were vital imports from North Africa. Oyo had a large army of soldiers who were skilled at fighting from horseback. This fearsome cavalry allowed Oyo to conquer and expand during the 15th and 16th centuries.

Oyo's kings were called *alafins*. The *alafins* led Oyo to its height during the 17th and 18th centuries. But, unlike other Guinea states, Oyo did not use European firearms until the 19th century and had few direct dealings until then with Europeans and the Atlantic slave trade.

By 1800, Oyo was fragmenting – with chiefs and officials challenging the *alafin's* power. Oyo's southern states, such as Dahomey, grew richer and more powerful until, eventually, they broke away. The Fulani (see page 21) were threatening from the north, preventing horses from reaching the Oyo cavalry. Civil war broke out in Oyo. But in the middle of the 19th century, the Yoruba developed a new state – Ibadan and many new towns.

2. Benin

Benin emerged some time between the 10th and 14th centuries AD. Like Oyo, its people saw Ile Ife as their spiritual and cultural source. The people of Benin were known as Edo, and they called their kings *oba*. Through the *oba*, the empire expanded and prospered until the 19th century. Even states not

A CLOSER LOOK

The original state of the Yoruba people was Ife, with its capital Ile Ife. Long after its decline, this ancient capital continues to be a spiritual homeland for the Yoruba people. Legend has it that Ile Ife was founded by Oduduwa, the father of all Yoruba peoples. When Oduduwa lay dying, he summoned his 16 sons to his side. He urged them to go out and create new kingdoms. On their heads he placed beaded crowns which are worn by Yoruba kings to this very day.

This 13th-century, bronze-cast head represents either an Ife king, or Olokun, the sea-goddess.

Portuguese traders or officials are depicted on this 17th-century bronze plaque from Benin.

directly under Benin's control looked to Benin for approval.

Benin is distinguished from the other West African states by its early and sustained contact with the Portuguese. Controlling the entry of Europeans through a single port, Ughoton, Benin managed to trade successfully, yet limit European influence. The *oba* sent ambassadors to the Portuguese court in Lisbon – but this, too, failed to secure for Portugal a confident foothold in Benin.

Benin's slow decline began in the 18th century. This was as a result of internal rivalries and the loss of trade to other states, particularly small coastal states and Dahomey. Its vassal states began to break away. The British sacked and looted Benin in 1897, resulting in many of its treasures being taken off to European museums.

3. Dahomey

The Aja people of Dahomey had once lived in the savannah, in present-day Ghana, but they migrated southwards in the early 16th century. They were related to the Yoruba of Oyo and to the Edo of Benin.

The Aja kingdoms formed a stable state until Europeans began competing for trade, establishing

A CLOSER LOOK

The kingdom of Nupe, ruling over people of the same name, began in the 10th century, possibly even earlier. It sat just north of the Niger and Benue rivers – between the savannah and the forest. Its rulers were known as the *Etsu Ede*. They were very powerful, but they were greatly influenced by royal women, particularly their sisters.

Throughout most of its history, Nupe was continually under attack from Oyo and the Hausa states, all of which required Nupe to pay tribute to them. But despite its precarious position, Nupe was never completely swallowed up by other states until it became part of the Islamic Fulani Empire (see page 21) in the 19th century.

trading posts along the coast. This caused rivalry amongst the Aja. It was in the midst of this turmoil that Dahomey was formed in about 1625. By the 18th century, the Dahomey Empire covered the forest and coastland of what is now the Republic of Benin. However, Dahomey became overshadowed by its powerful neighbour, Oyo, which tried to invade Dahomey several times. In order to fight off Oyo, the government of Dahomey needed firearms which it could get only by entering into the slave trade. This it did reluctantly, knowing that the transportation of slaves would take valuable labour away from the region. And despite the new-found supply of weapons, the people of Dahomey were still eventually forced to pay tribute to Oyo.

In the 19th century, Dahomey became the most powerful empire in the Guinea region. Four strong leaders ensured that Dahomey kept its power until the end of the 19th century.

This gold head once belonged to an emperor of Asante. It may represent the face of a defeated enemy.

4. Asante

The Asante kingdom of the Akan people developed west of the River Volta in the 16th century. It was originally a gold-producing kingdom, but it adapted to the lucrative trans-Atlantic slave trade which enabled it to extend its power in the 17th century. Like many Guinea forest states, it aimed to push its borders to the coastline to stop coastal states from controlling the trade with the Europeans.

Asante's first leader was Osei Tutu (1660-1712). Osei Tutu created a focus for his subjects' loyalty and devotion. This focus was his throne – the Golden Stool (see page 30) which became a symbol of the *Asantehene's* (king's) power.

Under another great king, Opoko Ware (1721-50), Asante became the greatest empire on the Gold Coast. But by the 19th century, disputes about who should be the next *Asantehene* led to civil war. The coastal states regained their strength, helped by European traders who were backed by their governments. In the 19th century, Asante put up a brave fight against the British colonialists. Even after their defeat and the exile of their king, Prempeh, the people of Asante pressurised the British into reinstating the *Asantehene*, in 1935.

5. Niger Delta States

Many small states formed among the maze of creeks and waterways of the Niger Delta. Among the several eastern states peopled by the Ijo was Bonny. As early as the 12th century, Bonny and its neighbouring states developed from trading towns dealing in agricultural produce into small trading states. At first, these states traded with the other states further inland and with Benin to the west.

During the 17th and 18th centuries, the Delta states became the most important trading centres for the trans-Atlantic slave trade – giving the Slave Coast its name. The network of swamps and creeks made transportation perilous for Europeans, but easy for local people. As a result, these states thrived on organising trade between the Europeans and the peoples of the interior.

The 19th century saw a dramatic change in the Delta area – from trade in slaves to trade in locally grown palm oil (see page 16). Now known as the Oil Rivers states, the old slave-trading states were able to adapt and maintain their importance in the region until, eventually, their European trading partners were replaced by colonial rulers.

A CLOSER LOOK

King Jaja was the king of the state of Bonny until he set up the rival trading state called Opobo. King Jaja made Opobo one of the largest centres for the export of palm oil in the Delta. He maintained good relations with the Europeans, being the first king in the area to help shipwrecked sailors. But from the 1870s, King Jaja recognised the threat of European colonialism. In 1873, he signed a treaty with the British. This treaty gave King Jaja the power to stop European traders from establishing trading posts near his territory. However, the king's continued resistance to the British led to his arrest in 1887, and he was exiled to the West Indies, where he died.

THE IMPORTANCE OF RELIGION

Religion played an important part in all the states of West Africa. It bound peoples together, and it gave a focus for daily life. And although important in itself, religion cannot be separated from the politics or economics of the states.

Historical evidence gives us some idea of religious practices in West African societies at particular times. But in none of the West African states are changes in beliefs and practices fully documented.

Some of the evidence for traditional religions comes from the study of ancient artefacts. The problem with this is that the significance of an artefact is often lost over the ages. Another source is the study of more recent or current religious

A sculpted shrine in the Nigerian countryside

practices. But these, too, can change over time both in the way they are performed and in their meaning.

The adoption of other religions, particularly Islam and Christianity, altered the role of traditional religions in many communities. Similarly, traditional religions affected the way Islam and Christianity were practised. For example, ancient, traditional ceremonies have often been incorporated into Islamic and Christian feast days.

Written accounts provide another source. There are often many problems with these accounts, particularly an observer's lack of understanding, and influences from his or her own religious background. One example of such an account is by Archibald Dalziel, a British trader. In the late 17th century, Dalziel collected eyewitness descriptions of life in Dahomey. This passage reports on traditional religion in the royal court of Dahomey. It reflects the European, Christian bias of Dalziel while leaving us unclear about the actual religious practices in Dahomey of the time: 'With respect to the Dahoman religion, it will hardly be expected that we should be able to say much. Like that of many other countries, it consists of a jumble of superstitious nonsense, of which it is impossible to convey any satisfactory idea to the reader.'

This portrait of Olaudah Equiano was painted in England in the 1780s.

TRADITIONAL BELIEFS

People in Dahomey and other non-Muslim, West African societies believed in a Supreme Being – a creator and intellectual force. God was often symbolised by the sun, moon, animals or trees and was reached through prayer and thanksgiving, much as in other major world religions.

A sympathetic witness to traditional beliefs in West Africa was Olaudah Equiano. Equiano was born around 1745 in an outlying district of the Benin kingdom. He was the son of an Ibo elder, but was captured as a slave and taken to Maryland, USA. He bought his own freedom, had many adventures, and while living in England he fought against the slave trade and wrote his autobiography. His accounts give an insight into life in a region uncharted by Europeans until the 19th century. It is therefore very important. But it must be remembered that he left his home town when still a young boy, and memories can be unfaithful at times. This is what he said about religion in his home town: 'As to religion, the natives believe that there is one Creator of all things, and that he lives in the sun... They believe he governs events, especially our deaths or captivity; but, as for the doctrine of eternity, I do not remember to have ever heard of it: some however believe in the transmigration of souls to a certain degree. Those spirits, which are not transmigrated, such as their dear friends or relations, they believe always attend them, and guard them from the bad spirits of their foes.'

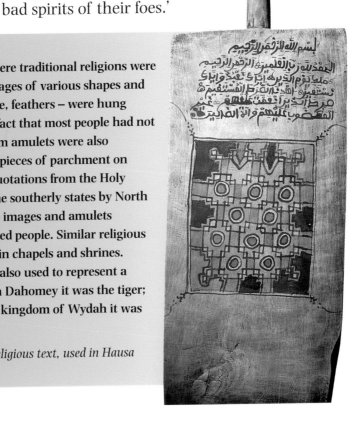

A CLOSER LOOK

In ordinary homes where traditional religions were practised, religious images of various shapes and materials – wood, bone, feathers – were hung inside. In spite of the fact that most people had not accepted Islam, Muslim amulets were also displayed. These were pieces of parchment on which were written quotations from the Holy *Qu'ran* , brought to the southerly states by North African traders. These images and amulets protected and comforted people. Similar religious symbols were housed in chapels and shrines. Certain symbols were also used to represent a nation's spirituality. In Dahomey it was the tiger; in the more southerly kingdom of Wydah it was the snake.

A wooden board with religious text, used in Hausa Muslim schools

This is the top of a carved staff showing Shango, the Yoruba god of thunder. The staff may have been carried by dancers during a religious ceremony.

Olaudah Equiano also describes the shrine of his dead grandmother, and the devotion of his mother in laying down offerings to her mother's spirit. The spirits of close relatives protected the family, as Olaudah said. Offerings of food and drink made the spirits feel loved and cared for.

THE POWER OF RELIGION

In the Guinea states, the king held great spiritual power. However, he did not have sole control over the state religion, which was managed by a powerful priesthood. In the Yoruba kingdom of Oyo, for example, the support and worship of many gods was highly organised. Gods included Obatala (the god of creativity), Ifa (knowledge), Shango (thunder), Oduduwa (earth), Oshun (water) and Yemoja (magic). Great political power was held by those who controlled the different religious groups. Indeed, by the 19th century, the Basorun (chief religious administrator) had so much power that Oyo slid into chaos (see page 36).

The *Asantehene* (kings) of Asante (see page 25) were well aware of the power of religion in their citizens' lives. *Asantehene* Osei Tutu strengthened his own kingship with the spiritual symbol of a throne known as the Golden Stool. It really was a golden stool, and Osei Tutu's people saw it as a

A CLOSER LOOK

In traditional religions, a dead person's spirit was considered powerful, and was treated with great respect. This was demonstrated particularly at funerals – and especially a king's funeral. In 16th-century Benin, a Portuguese pilot wrote this account: 'They [the Benin people] worship the sun, and believe that spirits are immortal, and that after death they go to the sun... When the king dies, the people all assemble in a large field, in the centre of which is a very deep well... They cast the body of the dead king into this well and those who are judged to have been most dear to and favoured by the king... go down to keep him company. When they have done so, the people place a great stone over the well and remain by it day and night.'

THE IMPORTANCE OF RELIGION

The King of Asante sits on the Golden Stool. He is shaded by a richly decorated parasol, another symbol of authority.

representation of the *Asantehene's* religious and political power. The stool united the Asante and gave them a sense of their own power as a nation. This, however, fell apart in the late 18th century. At this time, the Asante Empire was so huge that it included many different peoples. They held their own beliefs and felt no loyalty to the *Asantehene* in his far-off capital, let alone his throne. It was this lack of spiritual and political unity that finally led the Asante Empire to crumble.

In the Delta states, the king was also the high priest – the guardian of the nation's beliefs. But inland from the Niger Delta, the power of religion was not confined to courts and kings. Religious power was well used by the Aro Ibo people of the inland Delta states, where there were no powerful king-like figures. Particularly during the trans-Atlantic slave trade, Aro traders were protected by the Aro-Chuku oracle. The oracle was a spiritual force with powers to advise and help people. Its 'home' was a shrine where people came to make their appeals for assistance and blessing. The priests of the oracle accepted offerings on behalf of the spirit, and delivered its judgement. It was believed that people who ignored the judgement of the oracle would perish. The Aro-Chuku oracle and its priests were thought to be so powerful that Aro traders were allowed to pass from the coast to the Ibo communities in the interior without any problems.

THE IMPACT OF ISLAM

Long before the 15th century, Islam penetrated the Sudanic states from North Africa, making Islam the religion of the ruling classes and intellectuals. The Guinea states, too, were influenced by Muslim traders from North Africa. Mali produced some of

Islamic design mixed with traditional West African architecture to produce some of the most stunning mosques in the Muslim world. This mosque is in Burkina Faso.

West Africa's most prominent early Muslim leaders, such as Mansa Musa (see page 18). The poor people of Mali kept mainly to traditional beliefs and practices, although converts to Islam increased as Muslim traders brought their religion and education to outlying towns.

The invasion of Muslim Moors from North Africa in the 16th century strengthened the numbers of Muslims in western Sudan – but led to the downfall of Mali itself. However, it was the Fulani *jihads* of the late 18th and early 19th centuries that finally made Islam the dominant religion in this area (see page 21). Nevertheless, traditional practices blended in with those brought by Islam – as they did later with Christianity.

THE *BIBLE* AND THE GUN

Christians arrived in Benin as early as the 16th century. From the 18th century onwards, traders from the coastal states learned much about the cultures of their European counterparts, including

THE IMPORTANCE OF RELIGION

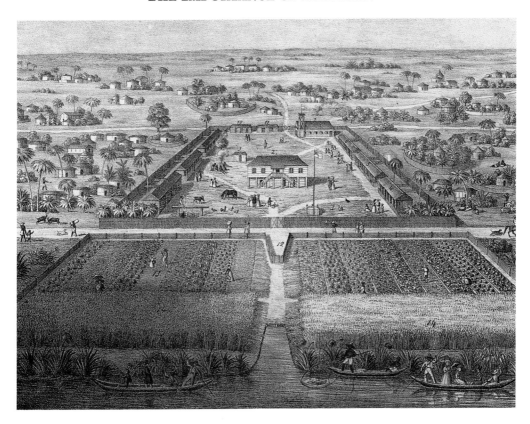

A view of an English mission station, with its own farm. It was built in Badagry, southern Nigeria, in about 1840.

their religion. Many of the traders' families became Christians. Some West African Christians visited Europe and saw the role and practice of Christianity there. In the early 19th century, missionary activity began in earnest along the coast. By the mid 19th century, missionaries from many European nations had set up mission stations, schools and hospitals in most of West Africa.

After the abolition of slavery (see page 47), some former slaves returned from the Americas to West Africa. They settled on the far west coast in Liberia. Others came from Britain to live in Freetown, Sierra Leone. Many of these people were Christians and some worked as missionary agents for, among others, the Church of England, helping to spread Christianity across West Africa.

In West African states, politics, military power and Christianity became inseparable in the late 19th century. The aggression of European companies and governments led to a reaction against the Christian faith in some communities.

However, this was by no means the end of Christianity in West Africa and, as a local Christian priesthood developed, the religion strengthened.

Christianity had other impacts upon West Africa. First, many of the new Christians were given a European education. They were employed by European traders, missionaries and administrators. European-educated Christians developed as a separate group, sometimes finding themselves in conflict with the traditional ruling groups.

A second political change to the region was that most Christian activity took place in the south. Islam's stronghold remained in the north. This religious division led to resentments and conflict. Under colonialism, northern Muslims and southern Christians within the same national boundaries often felt that colonial governments favoured either one or the other faith and region.

This traditional Ibo mask is decorated with a crest of Christ's crucifixion.

A CLOSER LOOK

One of the most influential priests in West Africa was Bishop Samuel Ajayi Crowther (1809-91) (right). He was a Yoruba, born in Oshogun, but was later captured as a slave and then rescued from a Portuguese slave ship in 1822. From there, Samuel Crowther was taken to Freetown, Sierra Leone where, in 1843, he was ordained as a priest in the Church of England. He was made Bishop of 'Western Equatorial Africa beyond the Queen's Dominions' in 1864. However, just after his death, the Church withdrew its policy of promoting West African clergy to senior positions. This led to a split in the Church and the separate, successful, development of a West African branch.

GOVERNING THE STATE

A traditional ruler is saluted by his people, officials and village leaders in modern-day Ghana. The huge parasol has long been a symbol of power and respect.

West African societies had many different types of political systems. In many states, a king and a huge number of court officials governed from a state capital. These officials administered large kingdoms and at times, vast empires. There were also many forms of social and political order in smaller states and societies. In some of these smaller states, there was a government with a king. In others, decisions were made collectively by councils.

BALANCING POWER

To many observers, it appeared that the kings of West African states held absolute authority. This was often the conclusion drawn from the elaborate court ceremonials, the riches held by royalty, and the obedience shown to kings by their officials (see page 40). In fact, kings could not do exactly as they pleased. As in Europe, officials put checks upon the behaviour and policies of their monarchs. However, strong, efficient leaders did have a better chance of respect and obedience from their ministers, and a longer life than weak, inefficient ones.

Oyo is a good example of the checks that were put on royal authority in the larger states. The *alafin* (king) of Oyo was selected by kingmakers among the

Asante elders wear decorated gold headgear to show their status.

chiefs. This meant that the *alafin* owed his power to them, which made his position rather insecure. But it also meant that there was little chance of Oyo's rulers becoming tyrants. In their turn, Oyo's chiefs were heads of prominent families, who owed their status more to their relatives and supporters than to the *alafin*. This meant that they had to bear in mind the wishes of their supporters.

In the 18th century, successive *alafin* were considered so weak in character – unable even to lead their troops into battle – that they were either poisoned or forced to commit suicide. At this time, the Basorun and the Kakanfo (chief of cavalry) rose

A CLOSER LOOK

Evidence from the end of the 17th century suggests that the political hierarchy in Oyo was made up of the *alafin* and the royal family, a council of senior chiefs (Oyo Misi), administrative officials (Asoju-obe meaning, 'one who has the king's eyes'), and a council of religious and political leaders (Ogboni). Various military commanders were made to compete with each other in warfare. This kept them on their toes – anxious to please the *alafin* who played them off against each other in order to maintain his authority. By the 18th and 19th centuries, the greatest power lay in the hands of the Basorun who was the chief administrator of the official religion.

to power above the *alafin*. It seems likely that weak *alafin* were chosen on purpose so that other officials could easily seize power.

Family ties

Among the kingdoms of the Aja people to the west of Oyo, rulers and administrators were linked through lineage (family) ties. This provided stability both within the kingdoms and between kingdoms. Rulers and administrators from different kingdoms peacefully consulted each other when problems arose. This system fell apart when European traders arrived on the scene, establishing coastal trading posts. The fierce competition for trade sparked intense rivalry among the kingdoms, breaking royal family ties.

Observing the havoc caused by family rivalries, the kings of the Aja state of Dahomey approached things differently. They established a meritocracy (where people are rewarded according to their worth) rather than a system based on family ties. In the royal court an individual was judged on loyalty and ability, and promotion was gained if these two qualities were judged to be strong.

At Elmina, in Ghana, young people carry a golden stool and other regal items as part of a ceremonial procession.

Dense, tropical vegetation covers much of the coast of West Africa.

AWAY FROM THE STATE

Some West African societies have never been organised into states. From modern-day Guinea round to Côte d'Ivoire, large-scale state expansion was hampered by dense forest and a long, torrential rainy season. Contact with peoples beyond the forest to the north was limited, although refugees from the Sudanic states sometimes found their way to this safe area.

There were many parts of West Africa, even within states, where social organisation was on a small scale. Particularly in societies that occupied the region of present-day southern Nigeria, decisions were made collectively by groups of village or town elders. There were often several tiers of elder, the more senior and those with most titles being the most influential. Often a senior elder held the deciding vote in matters of dispute.

A CLOSER LOOK

The elders made up the top layer of a complex system of organisation. Mostly, the structure was based on males who were grouped into age grades. Throughout their lives, boys and men of each grade had a level of responsibility. Every type of communal work, such as house-building and harvesting, was carried out by men belonging to a particular grade. Policing and carrying out the decisions of the elders were functions for men of middle years because they still enjoyed physical strength, yet had experience of life and the workings of their social system.

GOVERNING THE STATE

Even under such local systems there were power struggles. Some of these societies, recognising the authority of the far-off Benin court, at times asked the *oba* to confirm the position of elders. This suggests that there were occasional feuds and insecurities. It also gives an idea of the powerful influence of empires such as Benin, even beyond their boundaries.

POLITICS IN THE DELTA STATES

In the 15th century, the smallest unit within the Delta Ijo communities was the Ibe, or clan, which occupied a village. Members of the clan could trace their ancestry back to a common ancestor – a founding father. The sons of this ancestor then started new branches of the clan in outlying towns and villages. Even when other peoples, such as the Ibo, migrated to the central and western part of the Delta, they became absorbed into the system. Their loyalty to the Ijo leadership became part of their culture, too.

This system was strengthened by each clan's belief in the Ijo's national god, coupled with respect for the high priest who administered the national religion. On the eastern Delta, village gods were probably almost as important as the national god. They were linked to the national god rather than subject to him. This meant that new immigrants could bring their own deity into the system and it would be just one of many village gods linked to the national god. In this way, newcomers kept their own identities but forged links with other communities in the clan.

SECRET STRENGTH

There were many secret societies in West Africa. They were not secret in any mysterious sense – rather their membership was limited. Many of these societies were formed within religious groups, women's groups or age grades. They were very similar to craftsmen's guilds or the Freemasons in Europe. And, just as in Europe, many of these societies tried to ensure economic and political advancement for their members. Some secret societies were extremely powerful. The Efik Society of Calabar is one example.

East of the Delta states flows the Cross River. Here, in the 17th century, the four main settlements of the Efik people became the main trading towns serving the Atlantic slave trade. Together, the towns formed the state of Calabar. Membership of the Efik Society of Calabar was very important for kings and leaders of Efik lineages. To maintain their power, these kings and leaders had to belong to the highest grades within the Society – and they had to pay for the privilege. Marrying into a high-grade lineage was also encouraged. The Society had an important economic role setting out trading regulations with Europeans. And although Europeans paid trade duties directly to the kings, the wealth was then spread out among other members of the Efik ruling classes.

These linked brass staffs were made over 100 years ago. They were symbols of office for senior members of a secret society – the Yoruba Ogboni Society.

LIFE IN THE PALACE

Written accounts by foreign observers make it quite clear that the royal courts of West African empires were fabulous in their riches. Kings were treated with total obedience and dedication, and palace officials were in awe of their king.

To get a taste of court life, we can look at Dahomey in the 18th century. The king was treated with complete deference. No one was allowed to sit in the king's presence, except chosen women. Even the prime minister, on entering the palace gate, was expected to remove his silk clothes and put on a simple cotton tunic and trousers. A necklace of coral was hung around his neck and silver bracelets around his wrists. A sword was slung in a silver hilt at his side and in his hand he clutched an ivory mace – an expensive item made from a whole

The late Oba Akenzua II of Benin is clothed in coral robes and jewellery. The use of coral links the ruler of Benin with Olokun, the goddess of the sea.

elephant's tusk. As he approached the throne room, one of the women from the king's retinue signalled permission for the prime minister to enter. He then threw himself on the ground, crawled on his hands and knees towards the king and uttered expressions of obedience.

Ministers had many privileges and great wealth. But this wealth could not include goods reserved for the king, such as sandals or a royal parasol – a great and practical symbol of importance. Neverthless, ministers dressed in fine clothes, had their own, lesser kinds of parasol, and were attended to by an enormous retinue of servants and slaves. They were fêted by flags, drums and trumpets. And even the king's sons were expected to salute ministers by kneeling down before them and clapping their hands. These customs were elaborate – but hardly more so than in European courts of the time.

41

TRADE, TAXES AND TRIBUTE

The flow of trade between the Guinea and Sudanic states of West Africa (see page 13) helped many of these states to expand. However, trading goods was only one form of income – taxing goods and exacting tribute were others.

This terracotta figure is 700 years old. It is from Mali and shows a rich man on his horse – a symbol of wealth brought about by trade.

DIRECT AND INDIRECT TRADE

Most states conducted some direct trade with other West African or North African states and, later, with European traders. For example, Mali exchanged copper for goods from the Guinea states. States also conducted indirect trade – they acted as middlemen. Mali was middleman between the southern Guinea states and the states of North Africa, raising money by taxing goods such as gold and kola nuts before they passed out of the state.

The economy of Oyo rested partly on collecting dues from its vassal states. Its other income was drawn from acting as a middleman between the northern Sudanic states such as the Hausa, and states such as Benin to the south. For Oyo, the most important direct imports from the Hausa states were horses and saddles, which allowed Oyo to form the most organised and feared cavalry in the region.

Near the coast, Ijo towns and villages in the Niger Delta originally traded directly with each other. People from the saltwater settlements exchanged fish for agricultural products grown by farmers from the freshwater swamp areas further inland. Gradually, the expanding states began to trade with neighbouring peoples of the western Delta, such as the Benin Empire. Agricultural produce and slaves were brought by huge canoes from the interior to the coastal areas along the network of waterways. The Ijo used salt as an exchange for these goods. They extracted the salt from the roots of mangrove trees.

During the 16th century, the role of the trading states as middlemen increased, and the Delta states grew rich on this. Slaves and produce from the interior were collected at the Delta trading stations and sold on to Europeans. In turn, the Delta states sold European goods to the peoples of the interior. This trade developed during the 17th and 18th centuries, with slaves being the main commodity. So huge was the part played by the Delta States in the trans-Atlantic slave trade that this stretch of coast became known to Europeans as the Slave Coast. From the 1830s, the now illegal slave trade was largely replaced with legitimate trade in palm oil (see page 16).

A steamboat arrives at the trading station of Iddah on the lower Niger River in the 1890s.

A CLOSER LOOK

In many parts of West Africa, every town and village held local markets in the morning and evening. Larger markets, often lasting several days or even a couple of weeks, attracted people from further afield. Barter was not the only form of exchange. Currencies were used long before the 15th century. Manilla, cowry, metal ring and coin currencies have all been found in the Niger Delta region. A manilla was a metal bracelet, often made in a horseshoe shape (see right). Manillas were used to the east of the Niger Delta. The cowry shell (right) was the currency of the Yoruba of Oyo and the Aja of Dahomey. To the west, among the Asante, the currency was gold and gold dust.

EUROPEAN TRADE

Prince Henry of Portugal was known as Henry the Navigator because of his interest in exploration by sea.

The first goods from West Africa to reach Europe came through contact with North Africa – especially through the North African Moorish empires in Spain and Portugal. As Spain and Portugal freed themselves from Moorish control, from the 13th century onwards, they began to trade in African goods for themselves. In the 15th century, Prince Henry of Portugal funded and supported many voyages for exploration and trade. Portugal's first major trading partner in West Africa was Benin, whose king allowed the Portuguese to set up a trading station. At first, Portugal wanted to buy raw materials such as gums, oils, black pepper and ivory from Benin. These goods were taken by the Portuguese to the Gold Coast where they were exchanged for gold. In return, Benin received firearms, copper and beads.

Portugal continued trading in these goods, plus a small number of slaves captured by sailors, from

TRADE, TAXES AND TRIBUTE

A plantation in the Caribbean. African slaves, including children, were forced to work long hours cutting sugar-cane.

the 1440s to the end of the 16th century. The biggest threat to this trade was competition from other European nations, particularly Spain. However, Spain was busy with its 'discoveries' in the 'New World' (see page 14). In the Treaty of Tordesillas of 1494, Spain made an agreement with Portugal to trade only in the Americas, if Portugal traded only in Africa and Asia. But towards the end of the 16th century, Portugal's monopoly on trade in Africa ceased when the Dutch released themselves from Spanish rule. The Dutch began to send ships to West Africa and, by the middle of the 17th century, France and England were trading for slave workers to supply the plantations in their new colonies in the Americas. In exchange, Benin, and later other states, received manufactured goods and yet more firearms.

A CLOSER LOOK

Historians often emphasise the huge numbers of weapons sold to the West African states by European traders. But Europeans brought a vast array of other manufactured goods, too. By the end of the 17th century the aristocracy and merchant classes of West Africa were buying tables, chairs, chests, walking canes, silver cutlery and cups, glassware, clothing, silk, velvet, carpets, beds and bedding. Many of these products found their way to the far corners of empires.

Most West Africans' understanding of slavery was based on the roles and treatment of slaves within their own societies. This is what Olaudah Equiano (see page 28) had to say about slavery in his own (Ibo) society: 'Those prisoners [of war] which were not redeemed or sold we kept as slaves: but how different was their condition from that of the slaves in the West Indies! With us [in Ibo society] they do no more work than other members of the community, even their master; their food, clothing, and lodging, were nearly the same as theirs.'

THE SLAVE TRADE

The slave trade in West Africa began long before the 15th century. Slaves were usually prisoners of war, captured during fighting between states. Many became the personal servants of royalty and the rich. These slaves were accorded rights and respect, and some gained influential positions, wealth and land.

The number of slaves increased with the spread of Islam – and rocketed with the growth of the trans-Atlantic slave trade in the 17th century. The huge numbers of people taken to be slaves in the Americas devastated the interior of West Africa. The young, fit and healthy were obviously the most prized captives. The loss to their own societies was incalculable. Agriculture, industry, skills and technical progress were all hindered. The slave trading states became dependent on European firearms and manufactured goods. At the same time, the slaves and raw materials exported from West

Shackled slaves are forced on to a slave ship bound for the Americas.

TRADE, TAXES AND TRIBUTE

Africa helped to start a successful Industrial Revolution in Europe (see pages 16 and 58).

We will never know the exact numbers of slaves removed from West Africa during the centuries that witnessed the Atlantic trade. Many died on their way to the coast, and many more perished in transit to the 'New World'. It is probable that at least 20 million people were taken from the whole of Africa and transported to the Americas to work as slaves.

By the end of the 18th century, Europe started to withdraw from the slave trade, leaving the economies of West African slave trading nations in ruins. In 1807, it was made illegal for British subjects to take part in the slave trade. In 1814, the United States also declared the slave trade illegal. Although the campaign against slavery was well fought, there was, in any case, a decline in the demand for slaves in the Americas. This was partly because the African American population had increased. But it was also because European powers were looking to West Africa for other commercial reasons – to establish plantations on West African soil (see page 16). The slave trade did not come to a complete halt, even at this point. In Brazil and Cuba, the demand for slaves actually increased. So trans-Atlantic slave trading continued until 1888.

After the abolition of the slave trade in Britain, British naval ships patrolled the coast of West Africa to prevent other countries taking part in the slave trade. This picture shows a British naval vessel, the Pluto, *capturing a large slave ship.*

DAILY LIFE

Much of the evidence for daily life in West Africa comes from written accounts which provide detailed snapshots of particular places at certain times. This means that we have no overall picture of the gradual changes that took place over the centuries.

TOWN AND COUNTRY

Houses and thatched grain stores in a Dogon village in Mali. Building, thatching and craftwork are all dry-season occupations, when harvesting has been completed.

Travellers in the dry northern states of West Africa came across walled Hausa cities with narrow streets. The houses were quite large, square structures, packed closely together with a maze-like pattern of rooms and corridors which led into open courtyards. Outside, among vast acres of guinea-corn and millet fields, smaller village homes and cornstores on stilts were made from sun-dried clay, dung and straw bricks, with thatched roofs.

DAILY LIFE

Far to the west, the square, flat-roofed houses with small windows reminded many travellers of buildings on the Mediterranean coast. Further south, deep in the forest states, canes were used to support thatched roofs and, in some areas, palm leaves for shading verandahs. High walls or fencing surrounded large family compounds, where several houses were grouped together.

A wealthy, young Mali woman in 19th-century dress

FASHIONS

There were as many different styles of dress in West Africa as there were societies. Long before the 15th century, cotton and hemp cloth were woven and dyed in West Africa. With the coming of European trade, imported silks and satins became fashionable for the rich. As for footwear, the Hausa had been exporting fine dyed and patterned leather sandals for hundreds of years.

In the 1820s, a British trader, John Adams, observed dress in the court of Benin: 'The King and his principal courtiers are ostentatious in their dress, wearing damask, taffity [taffetta], and cuttanee [a fine linen from the East Indies]... Coral is a very favourite ornament... and the women... wear a profusion of beads...'

In the 17th century, ordinary women in parts of the Guinea region wore skirts down to their calves, hair curled round their heads like garlands, one half coloured black and the other red, and copper bracelets on their arms. Bracelets, beads, amulets and other religious symbols were commonly worn as jewellery in many of the states. Elaborate hair plaiting was a striking feature.

The dye pits of Kano are a series of cemented holes dug into the ground.

In the rural areas of the Ibo, in the 18th century, Olaudah Equiano describes dress as being fairly uniform and made from blue, cotton cloth. For hundreds of years, blue was the colour of many garments in the Hausa states, too. In Kano, there were dye pits dug into the ground. Turbans were dyed a deep blue, then beaten until the cloth developed a silvery sheen. This tradition continues today.

FOOD AND FARMING

People in West Africa grew a huge variety of crops, and there was an abundance of livestock and fish. From the 17th century onwards, these local supplies were supplemented by foodstuffs from the Americas and Europe.

Net-fishing on the River Niger at Mopti, in Mali

The Ijo people of the Niger Delta swamps used poisons extracted from fruit seeds to stun both saltwater and freshwater fish. The fish were then caught using basket traps. In the freshwater swamp areas, yams, bananas and plantains were cultivated. Trade with the interior supplied cattle, goats, sheep, hogs, chickens, palm oil and palm wine. These goods were transported in huge canoes built from single tree trunks along the maze of waterways. With European trade in the 17th century came produce such as cassava, maize, potato, tomato and other vegetables from Europe and the Americas.

In states such as Nupe and Oyo, maize, millet, or Guinea-corn were the staple grains. Kidney beans, groundnuts, yams and cassava were grown. People also harvested tropical fruits such as bananas, pineapples and melons.

Dalziel (see page 28) reported on cash-cropping – growing crops for sale – in 18th-century Dahomey: 'Nor is it [Dahomey] destitute of productions adapted for commerce and manufacture; such as indigo, cotton, the sugar-cane, tobacco, palm oil, together with a variety of spices, particularly a species of pepper... scarcely distinguishable from the black pepper in the East Indies.'

Travellers to West Africa also noted farming techniques. If you travel to West Africa today, you might notice two striking differences in cultivation techniques from those in Europe. The first is that the crops are often grown in mounds, or highly heaped ridges with deep furrows between them. The furrows retain moisture, and water is absorbed more directly by the root systems of the plants. The second difference is that there is a considerable amount of intercropping – different crops grown together in the same row in order to make good use of the space. Dalziel recorded these practices over 200 years ago.

In the dry savannah region, small patches of naturally damp land are used mainly for growing vegetables, especially tomatoes, peppers, greens and onions.

WOMEN

Until the 19th century, most written evidence about West Africa was supplied by male traders and explorers. None of them really concentrated on the role of women in society – it was crucial neither to their business operations nor to their own personal picture of the area. Nevertheless, there were a few interesting observations.

The role of women in royal circles was often one of great influence. Many queen mothers were kingmakers, with their own separate court and set of officials. In Dahomey, the king was officially outranked by the queen mother. All Dahoman officials had a female counterpart, who held a higher status in court. Some queen mothers, such as those in Asante, became temporary monarchs when no king could be enthroned. The Nupe king's sister was a very forceful adviser to her brother.

In the rest of Nupe society, and among many Ibo communities, ordinary women were also quite

A Fulani woman fetches water. Many women in West African societies work the land as well as doing the household chores.

powerful. Unusually, land was inherited through women, and they remained based in their home village or town even after they were married. According to Olaudah Equiano, in the outlying regions Ibo women led a very varied life, one minute spinning cotton and the next preparing to defend their communities in battle against raiders.

In Dahomey, it was a woman from the king's retinue of concubines and slaves who bore permission from the king to enter his court (see page 41). In many states, women had an even greater role than this – there were whole armies of them! European visitors to the Dahomey court were expected to review a female guard of honour, which they clearly found rather surprising. Even more shocking to Europeans was that these women were active soldiers, just like their male counterparts. This is Dalziel's description of the court of Dahomey in the 18th century:

'Within the walls of the different royal palaces in Dahomey are immured not less than *three thousand* women. Several hundreds of these are trained to the use of arms, under a female general and subordinate officers, appointed by the king, in the same manner as those under the Agaow [male general]. These warriors are regularly exercised, and go through their evolutions with as much expertness as male soldiers. They have their large umbrellas, their flags, their drums, trumpets, flutes and other musical instruments.'

A CLOSER LOOK
In the late 18th century, the Muslim leader Uthman dan Fodio (see page 21) had some harsh things to say about the treatment of women in the Hausa states. But it must be remembered that it was in Uthman dan Fodio's interests to criticise Hausa society and to spell out the good reasons for his invasion of the area, and the reform of Islam: 'Most of our educated men leave their wives, their daughters and their captives morally abandoned, like beasts, without teaching them what God prescribes should be taught them... Thus they leave them ignorant of the rules regarding ablutions, prayer, fasting, business dealings and other duties... Men treat these beings like household implements which become broken after long use and which are then thrown out on the dung-heap.'

ARTS AND CRAFTS

A wealth of visual arts and crafts were developed by West African societies. Wooden masks, wood and metal sculptures, patterned body scarring, painting, textiles, copper and bronze jewellery, pottery and architecture represent many aspects of the different cultures found in the region. Some of these art forms were made purely for their decorative beauty, others had religious or political significance.

This 16th-century ivory mask is from Benin. It was worn on a belt, like the one shown on page 41.

In Nupe, highly skilled craftsworkers produced some of the finest copper, leather, ceramic and textile wares found in West Africa. The workers, like their European counterparts during this period, were organised into craft guilds. These guilds looked after the interests of the workers, maintained standards and undertook training schemes. Benin had a similar system, and in Oyo artists were educated in community schools, serving several family compounds.

ROYAL RICHES

From the 16th century, palaces in Benin and Asante were elegantly designed and elaborately decorated. Decorations were made from a variety of rich materials – gold, bronze, ivory, glass and velvets made from raffia. Inside the huge palace at Benin, during its height in the 17th and 18th centuries, rooms were filled with polished bronze statues and wall plaques. Bronze ceremonial heads and sculptures were placed on altars. All of these objects were symbols of power and wealth.

ART AND RELIGION

Art was especially important in religion. Just as mosques, temples and churches have always contained beautiful images and decoration, so too did chapels and shrines of traditional West African religions. In the Yoruba kingdom of Oyo, shrines contained ornate masks, sculpted figures, pottery, rich cloths and jewellery in honour of the gods. Each god, such as Shango, the god of thunder, or Ifa, the god of knowledge, had its own symbols, styles and construction techniques. These were used by followers of each god.

SOCIAL SYMBOLISM

Art was also used to depict the roles of different sections of society. Gallantry and chivalry were depicted by armed soldiers in pitched battle and knights on horseback. In Benin, the bronze plaques that decorated palace walls depicted battles, court ceremonies and meetings with foreign ambassadors, demonstrating the power and pomp of the aristocracy.

Ceremonial art was not just for the wealthy. Ordinary people held traditional masquerades and ceremonial dances in which the participants wore specific masks and robes. Sometimes these costumes illustrated different aspects of society. The Ijo of the Delta states used costume to portray certain human characteristics, such as laziness, incompetence and greed. Certain designs were also associated with harvest festivals. During their harvest celebrations, the Bambara created wooden headdresses, carved in

Art and religion come together in this Dogon iron figure, which would be placed on an altar in a family shrine.

the shape of elegant antelopes. Art was also used to indicate a person's place of origin. For example, Fulani women had dyed and patterned scars on their faces to show which clan they came from.

MUSIC AND DANCE

Songs – sung and chanted poetry – were more than just entertainment. In most of the states, the *griots* who performed songs were custodians of history, relating the legends of origin of peoples and states, of mighty rulers and glorious battles. Much like the European court jester, *griots* provided rulers with essential information. The thoughts of ordinary people and the intrigues of ministers found their way into these court musicians' songs.

Using lutes, drums, wind and brass instruments, musicians expressed language as well as melody through their instruments. Many West African languages are tonal. This means that high, low, rising and falling voice tones, as well as actual letter sounds, have meaning. People recognise certain words when instruments use different tones or slurs. Drums and trumpets are mostly used in this way. For example, today among the Hausa people, trumpeters warn people when a *Sarki* (a traditional regional ruler) is about to arrive. They blow two notes, one low, the other higher. The audience recognises that these mean, 'Ya zo' (low-high) – 'He is coming'.

A Bambara antelope mask

Benin drummers in the 16th century

ARTS AND CRAFTS

DANCE AND CEREMONY

Dance was, and still is, a feature of ceremony and celebration all over West Africa – particularly at harvest time. As they have done for centuries, the Bambara honour Chi Wara, the divine creator of agriculture, through masked dancing on the cultivated fields. Legend has it that Chi Wara buried himself deep in the earth as an act of sacrifice – much as farmers give up their lives toiling in the fields. The dances remind the workers of the act of Chi Wara and inspire them to carry on with their tasks.

Stag dancers perform at a Dogon festival in Mali. The headdresses worn by the dancers represent stags' horns.

CHAPTER TEN

TURMOIL AND TAKEOVER

During the 19th century, the slave trade came to an end and European nations, especially France and Britain, became more interested in using West Africa to provide raw materials for the growth of their Industrial Revolutions.

TREATIES AND TRICKERIES

The carved doors show a Yoruba king receiving Captain Ambrose, the first British official to visit Ikere-Ikiti in 1895. They were carved by Olowe of Ise, a renowned sculptor.

Following in the footsteps of the early missionairies, explorers, especially from Britain, France and Germany, paved the way for European trading companies. These companies attempted to make treaties with the West African coastal states in order to use or take over their land. In some cases, rulers misunderstood the contents of the treaties – in others, it seems that treaties were probably forged.

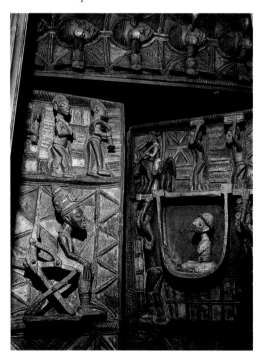

Those rulers who refused to make treaties were attacked by British and French government troops. Many of the soldiers involved in this action were, in fact, West African. The Europeans often chose troops who were traditional enemies of the particular state being attacked. These military operations ended in the defeat, but not necessarily the occupation, of many of the West African states.

These rather haphazard colonial activities led to the West Africa Conference in Berlin in 1884. Attended by European nations only, the conference officially approved colonial expansion in West Africa. According to the European nations, it gave them the right to attack and take over the region. The conference laid down rules by which each European power would accept the new African territories of the others.

The 'scramble for Africa' started. The French, initially wishing to develop plantations along the Senegal River, took over the river region near the coast and moved in on Segu in 1891. The southern coastal and Delta states were occupied by both British and French powers in the 1880s. The French moved north into Dahomey by 1894. The region once occupied by Oyo, Benin and Nupe was taken between 1888 and 1896 by the British, and the Hausa states finally collapsed when Sokoto, the capital of the eastern Fulani Caliphate, was defeated by the British in 1903. Ibo communities battled on until 1919. The colonial era proper had begun.

By the beginning of the 20th century, the ancient peoples and nations of West Africa were split by modern state boundaries. Many of the independent states discussed in this book now jostle together within the same national boundaries, imposed by European powers. Nevertheless, many of the titles, traditions, social structures, religious customs, art and music of the West African states still remain.

The French built this railway with a local labour force at Kayes in Mali in 1880, before their West African territories had even been recognised by other European powers. The British and Germans also undertook similar projects.

TIMELINE

AD

10th century	Mali has already begun large-scale social and political organisation. The Hausa states, Nupe, Oyo and Benin are just beginning.
12th century	Growth of Delta towns into small states
14th century	Mali, a key empire in the trans-Saharan trade, is at its height.
15th century	Mali begins a slow decline. Queen Amina of the Hausa state of Zaria extends the boundaries of Zaria city-state.
from 1440s	The West African coast is explored by Portuguese sailors and traders.
1486	Portuguese set up a trading station at the Benin port of Ughoton (Gwato).
1492	Christopher Columbus 'finds' the Americas – his 'discovery' is claimed by Spain, and the exploitation of the Americas begins.
16th century	Mali is invaded by Moors from North Africa, and declines rapidly. The Hausa states take over as important trans-Saharan trading states. Asante state forms. Benin expands. Nupe survives as a kingdom but pays tribute to both Oyo and Hausa states.
17th century	Expansion of Oyo, Asante and the Delta states. Dahomey state develops. Beginning of the Atlantic slave trade.
18th century	Growth of the Atlantic slave trade. Asante's rulers create a strong, centralised monarchy and expand their empire. The Delta states expand, largely due to involvement in the slave trade. Dahomey extends its boundaries, but is forced to pay tribute to Oyo. Benin begins to decline. Nupe suffers internal strife. Benin slowly slips into decline.
1790s	Beginning of the Fulani *jihads*. Dahomey fights off Oyo.
1800-70s	Yoruba wars and the Asante wars reflect internal strife in Oyo and Asante. Both empires fragment into smaller kingdoms and cities. Dahomey strengthens its position. Nupe, now under Fulani rule, expands.
1807	Abolition of slavery in Britain
1814	Abolition of slavery in USA
1820s	In the Delta states, palm oil begins to replace slaves as the principal commodity. European explorers and Christian missionaries arrive in the area. European trading companies follow, looking for raw materials and land treaties with local rulers.
1861	Segu is taken by the Fulani.
1865	Slavery is outlawed everywhere except Brazil and Cuba. European governments, especially the French and British, back traders with military force. West African territory is gradually taken over by European trading companies and governments.
1884	West Africa Conference in Berlin – European powers make rules of acceptance for each others' colonies in West Africa.
1888	Final abolition of slavery and the slave trade in Brazil.
1919	Ibo communities are finally defeated by the British. Colonialism begins.

GLOSSARY

age grades where people are grouped according to age, and perform certain functions associated with their particular group.

amulet quotations from the Holy *Qu'ran* or the *Hadith* written on small pieces of parchment. They were hung round people's necks to protect them from harm.

artefacts practical or decorative objects crafted by people.

caliphate a Muslim state under a leader known as a caliph.

cavalry soldiers on horseback.

chronicled given as an account of historical events, in order of time.

commodity a trade good.

compound a walled group of houses belonging to an extended family.

concubine an unmarried female partner of a king or minister. In West Africa, kings and ministers often had many wives and concubines.

cowry a shell belonging to the Cypraea family, used as a currency.

genealogy a history of a family, listing a family's ancestors.

griots West African singers and poets who recite historical events and genealogies.

Guinea states the states occupying the Guinea belt.

indigo a natural blue dye obtained from the leaves of the indigo plant.

jihad a Muslim holy war.

kingmaker a member of the royal family, or a minister, who has the authority to choose the next king.

lineage a line of descent from a single ancestor.

linguistic concerning language.

lost wax process a metal-casting process in which a wax model is made, a metal mould is formed around it, and the wax is then melted, leaving the metal model.

manilla a metal bracelet used as currency. It is usually horseshoe-shaped.

meritocracy a government in which ministers and others are chosen for their abilities, not for their wealth or connections.

middleman a trader who buys goods and then sells them at a profit.

missionary a priest dedicated to spreading his or her religion.

Moorish refers to North African Berber Muslims who, under different dynasties, ruled much of North Africa between the 8th and the 16th centuries.

oracle a powerful spiritual force. Its home was a shrine where people came to seek help and advice.

oral traditions histories that are passed on from one generation to the next.

plantations land used to grow commercial crops, such as sugar cane and tobacco.

potash a grey mineral rock used in cooking.

recitations, poems, songs and stories.

regicide the killing of a monarch.

revenue money collected by a government, often in the form of taxation.

social anthropology the study of human societies, their belief systems, family and political relationships, material culture, laws, etc.

Sudanic states the states occupying the Sudanic belt.

surpluses goods or money that are extra to ordinary needs.

tribute taxes of goods, crops and slaves demanded from a weak state by a more powerful one.

vassal states states that pay tribute to a more powerful state. The tribute is often in the form of crops.

INDEX